Citizens of a S

A Book of Postcards

POMEGRANATE ARTBOOKS / SAN FRANCISCO

Pomegranate Artbooks
Box 6099
Rohnert Park, California 94927

Pomegranate Europe Ltd.
Fullbridge House
Fullbridge
Maldon, Essex CM9 7LE
England

ISBN 0-87654-901-6
Pomegranate Catalog No. A828

Pomegranate publishes books of postcards on a wide range of subjects.
Please write to the publisher for more information.

n. a. goodman

The photographs in this book of postcards were taken by the sisters Frances Allen (1854–1941) and Mary E. Allen (1858–1941) of Deerfield, Massachusetts, between 1885 and 1920. The Allen sisters began their careers as schoolteachers, but when deafness dictated a change of profession, they turned to photography. Although their images depict activities common to a rural community, many scenes were staged to portray the olden days. Self-taught in their craft, the Allen sisters nevertheless achieved a remarkable degree of success; their photographs were soon in great demand as illustrations, frontispieces, and covers for numerous books and popular magazines.

As the nineteenth century came to a close and people became nostalgic for simpler times, Deerfield's eighteenth-century houses and rural setting made the town an ideal location for the Allen sisters' pictorial photographs. Frances and Mary Allen's photographs of their neighbors and farming community continue to have wide appeal for those curious about the customs of old-time New England.

Deerfield, Massachusetts, is still a quaint town. Many of its eighteenth- and nineteenth-century homes are open to the public under the auspices of Historic Deerfield, Inc. Frances and Mary Allen's collection of original platinum and gum prints, as well as their glass plate negatives, are preserved in Memorial Hall Museum, Pocumtuck Valley Memorial Association, Deerfield, Massachusetts.

Citizens of a Small Town

Come to Dinner! Lizzie Temple blowing the dinner horn
Photograph by Frances and Mary Allen, Deerfield,
Massachusetts, c. 1904

Pomegranate, Box 6099, Rohnert Park, CA 94927

Citizens of a Small Town

Thanksgiving pies being made in the Allen house bake oven
Photograph by Frances and Mary Allen, Deerfield,
Massachusetts, c. 1904

Pomegranate, Box 6099, Rohnert Park, CA 94927

Citizens of a Small Town

Dyeing cloth
Photograph by Frances and Mary Allen, Deerfield,
Massachusetts, c. 1900

Pomegranate, Box 6099, Rohnert Park, CA 94927

Citizens of a Small Town

The blacksmith George W. Shaw (1849–1927)
Photograph by Frances and Mary Allen, Deerfield,
Massachusetts, c. 1900

Pomegranate, Box 6099, Rohnert Park, CA 94927

Citizens of a Small Town

The stockings were hung by the chimney with care, in hopes that St. Nicholas soon would be there. . . .
Photograph by Frances and Mary Allen, Deerfield, Massachusetts, c. 1914

Pomegranate, Box 6099, Rohnert Park, CA 94927

Citizens of a Small Town

Members of the Deerfield Society of Blue and White
Needlework embroidering a bed cover
Photograph by Frances and Mary Allen, Deerfield,
Massachusetts, c. 1900

Pomegranate, Box 6099, Rohnert Park, CA 94927

Citizens of a Small Town

*Antiquarian George Sheldon (1818–1916) and young
neighbor Mark Allen in the doorway of the Sheldon homestead*
Photograph by Frances and Mary Allen, Deerfield,
Massachusetts, c. 1898

Pomegranate, Box 6099, Rohnert Park, CA 94927

Citizens of a Small Town

Caroline Ray (1823–1904) provided the Brick Church with flowers for fifty years
Photograph by Frances and Mary Allen, Deerfield, Massachusetts, c. 1900

Pomegranate, Box 6099, Rohnert Park, CA 94927

Citizens of a Small Town

*Ruth Root (1883–1934) and Helen (Childs) Boyden
(1883–1973) out for a stroll in Wapping*
Photograph by Frances and Mary Allen, Deerfield,
Massachusetts, c. 1890

Pomegranate, Box 6099, Rohnert Park, CA 94927

Citizens of a Small Town

Loading hay
Photograph by Frances and Mary Allen, Deerfield,
Massachusetts, c. 1900

Pomegranate, Box 6099, Rohnert Park, CA 94927

Citizens of a Small Town

*Mary Ann (Stebbins) Wright and her niece Mary Houghton
enjoying a visit in the south parlor of the Asa Stebbins house*
Photograph by Frances and Mary Allen, Deerfield,
Massachusetts, c. 1885

Pomegranate, Box 6099, Rohnert Park, CA 94927

Citizens of a Small Town

The children of William and Lucy Andrews sledding
Photograph by Frances and Mary Allen, Deerfield,
Massachusetts, c. 1905

Pomegranate, Box 6099, Rohnert Park, CA 94927

Citizens of a Small Town

The cobbler Philo Munn (1813–1895)
Photograph by Frances and Mary Allen, Deerfield,
Massachusetts, c. 1890

Pomegranate, Box 6099, Rohnert Park, CA 94927

Citizens of a Small Town

Carlos Allen and friend bringing home the Christmas tree
Photograph by Frances and Mary Allen, Deerfield,
Massachusetts, c. 1900

Pomegranate, Box 6099, Rohnert Park, CA 94927

Citizens of a Small Town

A fallen elm in Wapping
Photograph by Frances and Mary Allen, Deerfield,
Massachusetts, c. 1890

Pomegranate, Box 6099, Rohnert Park, CA 94927

Citizens of a Small Town

Children's book author Mary P. Wells Smith (1840–1930) in the doorway of the John Williams house at Deerfield Academy
Photograph by Frances and Mary Allen, Deerfield, Massachusetts, c. 1900

Pomegranate, Box 6099, Rohnert Park, CA 94927

Citizens of a Small Town

William Stebbins (1817–1897) sharpening his scythe
Photograph by Frances and Mary Allen, Deerfield,
Massachusetts, c. 1895

Pomegranate, Box 6099, Rohnert Park, CA 94927

Citizens of a Small Town

Western Massachusetts's first historical society, Memorial
Hall Museum (the former Deerfield Academy building)
Photograph by Frances and Mary Allen, Deerfield,
Massachusetts, c. 1904

Pomegranate, Box 6099, Rohnert Park, CA 94927

Citizens of a Small Town

Cutting seed potatoes in preparation for spring planting
Photograph by Frances and Mary Allen, Deerfield,
Massachusetts, c. 1900

Pomegranate, Box 6099, Rohnert Park, CA 94927

Citizens of a Small Town

The Pocumtuck Basket Makers weaving raffia baskets on the back porch of the Manse
Photograph by Frances and Mary Allen, Deerfield, Massachusetts, c. 1900

Pomegranate, Box 6099, Rohnert Park, CA 94927

Citizens of a Small Town

A link with the past: the Stebbins sisters Lenora, Mary, Louisa, Maria, and Lucy
Photograph by Frances and Mary Allen, Deerfield, Massachusetts, c. 1895

Pomegranate, Box 6099, Rohnert Park, CA 94927

Citizens of a Small Town

Margaret (Tombs) Jones (1821–1906) churning butter
Photograph by Frances and Mary Allen, Deerfield,
Massachusetts, c. 1900

Pomegranate, Box 6099, Rohnert Park, CA 94927

Citizens of a Small Town

Husking corn
Photograph by Frances and Mary Allen, Deerfield,
Massachusetts, c. 1900

Pomegranate, Box 6099, Rohnert Park, CA 94927

Citizens of a Small Town

The onion harvest being sorted by eastern European immigrant farmers
Photograph by Frances and Mary Allen, Deerfield, Massachusetts, c. 1914

Pomegranate, Box 6099, Rohnert Park, CA 94927

Citizens of a Small Town

A day off: Dennis Burnett (1859–1918) fishing
Photograph by Frances and Mary Allen, Deerfield,
Massachusetts, c. 1914

Pomegranate, Box 6099, Rohnert Park, CA 94927

Citizens of a Small Town

Josiah Allen (1814–1895) making cider applesauce
Photograph by Frances and Mary Allen, Deerfield,
Massachusetts, c. 1890

Pomegranate, Box 6099, Rohnert Park, CA 94927

Citizens of a Small Town

Quiet time
Photograph by Frances and Mary Allen, Deerfield,
Massachusetts, c. 1900

Pomegranate, Box 6099, Rohnert Park, CA 94927

Citizens of a Small Town

Funeral of the Reverend Edgar Buckingham (1812–1894)
in the Brick Church
Photograph by Frances and Mary Allen, Deerfield,
Massachusetts, c. 1894

Pomegranate, Box 6099, Rohnert Park, CA 94927

Citizens of a Small Town

Harriet (Carson) Wells (1871–1960) making Christmas wreaths
Photograph by Frances and Mary Allen, Deerfield,
Massachusetts, c. 1909

Pomegranate, Box 6099, Rohnert Park, CA 94927

Citizens of a Small Town

The nineteenth-century kitchen of the Thomas Dickinson house when the Wetheralds were in residence
Photograph by Frances and Mary Allen, Deerfield, Massachusetts, c. 1915

Pomegranate, Box 6099, Rohnert Park, CA 94927